JEAN HWANG CARRANT
PHOTOGRAPHY BY AKIKO IDA

# COOKIE
# LOVE

OVER 30 DELICIOUS
COOKIE RECIPES

*Hardie Grant*

BOOKS

# CONTENTS

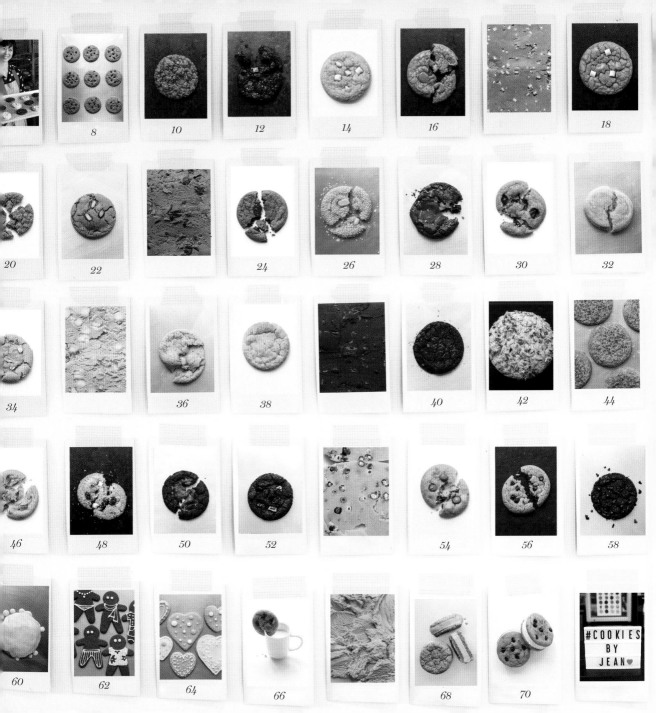

8

10

12

14

16

18

20

22

24

26

28

30

32

34

36

38

40

42

44

46

48

50

52

54

56

58

60

62

64

66

68

70

#COOKIES
BY
JEAN

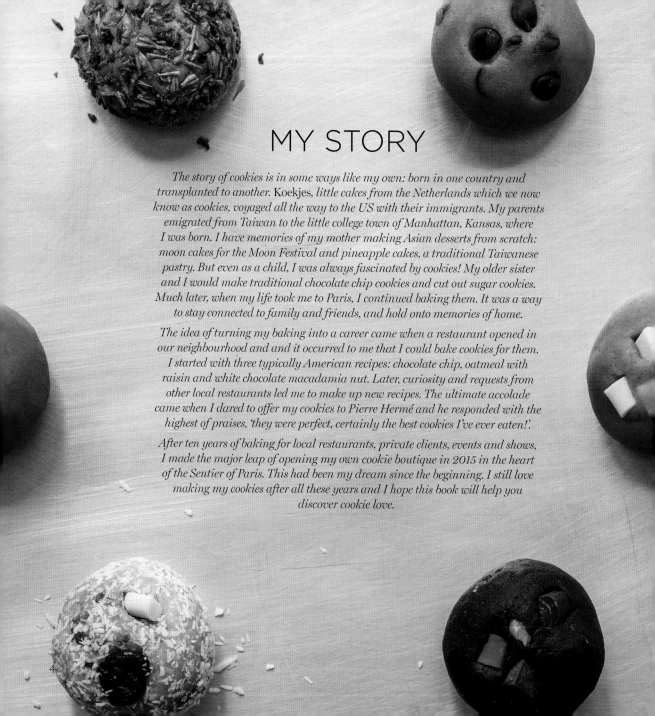

# MY STORY

*The story of cookies is in some ways like my own: born in one country and transplanted to another. Koekjes, little cakes from the Netherlands which we now know as cookies, voyaged all the way to the US with their immigrants. My parents emigrated from Taiwan to the little college town of Manhattan, Kansas, where I was born. I have memories of my mother making Asian desserts from scratch: moon cakes for the Moon Festival and pineapple cakes, a traditional Taiwanese pastry. But even as a child, I was always fascinated by cookies! My older sister and I would make traditional chocolate chip cookies and cut out sugar cookies. Much later, when my life took me to Paris, I continued baking them. It was a way to stay connected to family and friends, and hold onto memories of home.*

*The idea of turning my baking into a career came when a restaurant opened in our neighbourhood and and it occurred to me that I could bake cookies for them. I started with three typically American recipes: chocolate chip, oatmeal with raisin and white chocolate macadamia nut. Later, curiosity and requests from other local restaurants led me to make up new recipes. The ultimate accolade came when I dared to offer my cookies to Pierre Hermé and he responded with the highest of praises, 'they were perfect, certainly the best cookies I've ever eaten!'.*

*After ten years of baking for local restaurants, private clients, events and shows, I made the major leap of opening my own cookie boutique in 2015 in the heart of the Sentier of Paris. This had been my dream since the beginning. I still love making my cookies after all these years and I hope this book will help you discover cookie love.*

# COOKIE LOVE
# MAKING AND BAKING

## SECRET INGREDIENTS

**Brown sugar/muscovado sugar:** *this is a key ingredient for true American-style cookies! The sugar is slightly moist and gives the cookies a soft texture. The molasses content gives the dough a more complex flavour. If you leave the dough in the refrigerator to 'sleep' for one night before baking the cookies it creates an even better result.*

**Vanilla extract:** *American vanilla extract is alcohol-based. The recipes don't call for a lot, but I find that it adds a little punch to the dough. I make my own and it's very simple. Make the extract by slicing 6 vanilla pods (beans) in half lengthways, and then, if needed, cut them in half to shorten their length. Place them in a sealed glass container or bottle with 250 ml (8½ fl oz) of vodka and leave to macerate for at least 3 weeks, turning the container from time to time.*

**Flour:** *use the plainest plain (all-purpose) flour rather than fine pastry flour.*

## BAKING TIPS

*It's important not to over-bake the cookies! When they come out of the oven they may seem under-baked and many people put them back in to extend the baking time. Big mistake! When the cookies come out of the oven, leave them on the baking sheet for a few minutes to firm up. Then transfer them with a thin spatula to a baking rack to cool down. In order to make your cookies even more irresistible, add one of the ingredients in the batter (e.g. chocolate, nuts, dried fruit) onto the cookie when they are fresh out of the oven.*

# CHOC CHIP

preparation: 20 minutes + baking: 15 minutes

**makes 25 cookies**
225 g (8 oz/1 cup) slightly salted
   butter, at room temperature
200 g (7 oz/packed ¾ cup) dark or
   light brown sugar
90 g (3¼ oz/⅓ cup) caster
   (superfine) sugar
2 eggs
1 teaspoon vanilla extract
1 teaspoon bicarbonate of soda
   (baking soda)
1 teaspoon salt
400 g (14 oz/3 cups) plain
   (all-purpose) flour
120 g (4 oz/¾ cup) chocolate chips

Preheat the oven to 160°C (320°F/Gas mark 3).
Cream the butter and sugars until well blended. Add the
eggs, vanilla extract, bicarbonate of soda, salt and flour.
Once well combined, stir in the chocolate chips.
Form the dough into balls about the size of a golf ball
and space 7 cm (2¾ in) apart on a baking sheet.
Bake for 15 minutes. Leave the cookies to rest on the
baking sheet for 5 minutes and then allow to cool on a rack.

*This is the most traditional American cookie.*
*I am dedicating it to Arthur, aged 12, who fought bravely*
*against cancer. He loved simple chocolate chip cookies.*

# HALL & OATS

preparation: 20 minutes + baking: 15 minutes

**makes 25 cookies**
225 g (8 oz/1 cup) slightly salted
  butter, at room temperature
220 g (7¾ oz/packed ¾ cup) dark
  brown sugar
100 g (3¼ oz/½ cup) caster
  (superfine) sugar
2 eggs
1 tablespoon whole milk
1 teaspoon vanilla extract
250 g (9 oz/2 cups) plain
  (all-purpose) flour
200 g (7 oz/2 cups) rolled oats
1 teaspoon bicarbonate of soda
  (baking soda)
1 teaspoon salt
220 g (7¾ oz/1⅓ cups)
  golden raisins

Preheat the oven to 160°C (320°F/Gas mark 3).
Cream the butter and sugars until well blended. Incorporate
the eggs, milk and vanilla extract, then the flour, oats,
bicarbonate of soda and salt. When the dough is smooth,
stir in the raisins.
Form the dough into balls about the size of a golf ball and
space 7 cm (2¾ in) apart on a baking sheet.
Bake for 15 minutes. Leave the cookies to rest on the baking
sheet for 5 minutes and then allow to cool on a rack.

*This oatmeal cookie is my little tribute to 1980s music,
punning on the pop-rock duo of Daryl Hall and John Oates!*

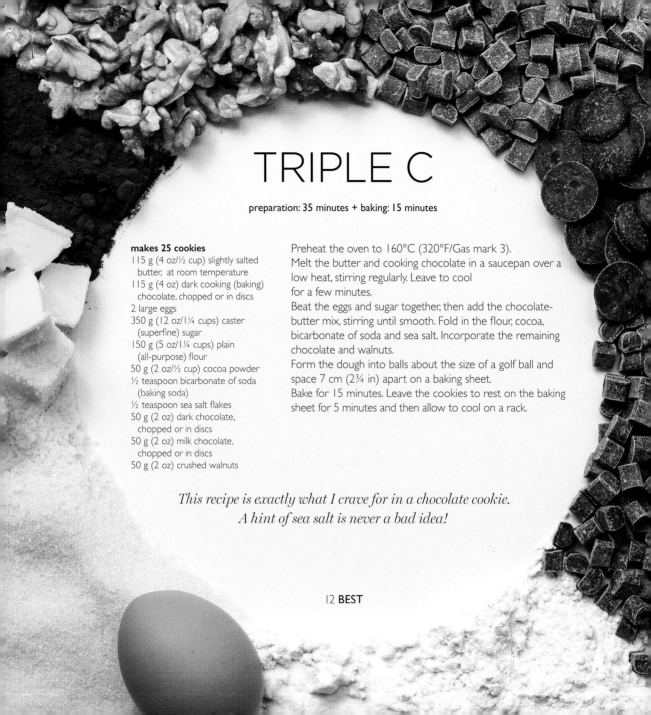

# TRIPLE C

preparation: 35 minutes + baking: 15 minutes

**makes 25 cookies**

115 g (4 oz/½ cup) slightly salted butter, at room temperature
115 g (4 oz) dark cooking (baking) chocolate, chopped or in discs
2 large eggs
350 g (12 oz/1¼ cups) caster (superfine) sugar
150 g (5 oz/1¼ cups) plain (all-purpose) flour
50 g (2 oz/½ cup) cocoa powder
½ teaspoon bicarbonate of soda (baking soda)
½ teaspoon sea salt flakes
50 g (2 oz) dark chocolate, chopped or in discs
50 g (2 oz) milk chocolate, chopped or in discs
50 g (2 oz) crushed walnuts

Preheat the oven to 160°C (320°F/Gas mark 3).
Melt the butter and cooking chocolate in a saucepan over a low heat, stirring regularly. Leave to cool for a few minutes.
Beat the eggs and sugar together, then add the chocolate-butter mix, stirring until smooth. Fold in the flour, cocoa, bicarbonate of soda and sea salt. Incorporate the remaining chocolate and walnuts.
Form the dough into balls about the size of a golf ball and space 7 cm (2¾ in) apart on a baking sheet.
Bake for 15 minutes. Leave the cookies to rest on the baking sheet for 5 minutes and then allow to cool on a rack.

*This recipe is exactly what I crave for in a chocolate cookie.*
*A hint of sea salt is never a bad idea!*

# MAC AND CHOC

preparation: 20 minutes + baking: 15 minutes

**makes 25 cookies**

225 g (8 oz/1 cup) slightly salted
    butter, at room temperature
200 g (7 oz/packed ¾ cup) light
    brown sugar
90 g (3¼ oz/⅓ cup)
    caster (superfine) sugar
2 eggs
1 teaspoon vanilla extract
400 g (14 oz/3 cups) plain
    (all-purpose) flour
1 teaspoon bicarbonate of soda
    (baking soda)
1 teaspoon salt
90 g (3¼ oz) white chocolate,
    chopped
30 g (1 oz) crushed macadamia
    nuts

Preheat the oven to 160°C (320°F/Gas mark 3).
Cream the butter and sugars until well blended. Incorporate
the eggs and vanilla extract, then the flour, bicarbonate of
soda and salt. When the dough is smooth, stir in the white
chocolate and macadamia nuts.
Form the dough into balls about the size of a golf ball
and space them about 7 cm (2¾ in) apart on a baking sheet.
Bake for 15 minutes. Leave the cookies to rest on the baking
sheet for 5 minutes and allow to cool on a rack.

*I took the name of this cookie from a play on words
with the famous 'Mac and Cheese' macaroni cheese. The white
chocolate-macadamia nut cookie is a fellow American classic!*

# GWENOLA

preparation: 20 minutes + baking: 15 minutes

**makes 25 cookies**
225 g (8 oz/1 cup) unsalted butter,
   at room temperature
100 g (3½ oz/packed ½ cup) dark
   brown sugar
100 g (3½ oz/packed ½ cup) light
   brown sugar
90 g (3¼ oz/⅓ cup) caster
   (superfine) sugar
2 eggs
1 teaspoon vanilla extract
400 g (14 oz/3 cups) plain
   (all-purpose) flour
1 teaspoon bicarbonate of soda
   (baking soda)
210 g (7½ oz) caramel milk
   chocolate, chopped
1 teaspoon coarse salt

Preheat the oven to 160°C (320°F/Gas mark 3).
Cream the butter and sugars until well blended. Incorporate
the eggs, vanilla extract, flour and bicarbonate of soda. When
the dough is smooth, stir in the chocolate and coarse salt.
Form the dough into balls about the size of a golf ball
and space them about 7 cm (2¾ in) apart on a baking sheet.
Bake for 15 minutes. Leave the cookies to rest on the baking
sheet for 5 minutes and then allow to cool on a rack.

*A cookie inspired by my Bikram yoga teacher, Gwen,*
*who requested this cookie because she's from Brittany – the*
*home of salted caramel. It's my hubby's favourite, too!*

# MATCHA BLANC

preparation: 20 minutes + baking: 15 minutes

**makes 25 cookies**

225 g (8 oz/1 cup) unsalted butter,
   at room temperature
200 g (7 oz/packed ¾ cup) light
   brown sugar
90 g (3¼ oz/⅓ cup) caster
   (superfine) sugar
2 eggs
400 g (14 oz/3 cups) plain
   (all-purpose) flour
6 g (3 teaspoons) matcha
1 teaspoon bicarbonate of soda
   (baking soda)
1 teaspoon salt
100 g (3¼ oz) white chocolate
   chopped or in discs

Preheat the oven to 160°C (320°F/Gas mark 3).
Cream the butter and sugars until well blended. Incorporate the eggs, flour, matcha, bicarbonate of soda and salt. When the dough is smooth, stir in the chocolate.
Form the dough into balls about the size of a golf ball and space them about 7 cm (2¾ in) apart on a baking sheet.
Bake for 15 minutes. Leave the cookies to rest on the baking sheet for 5 minutes and then allow to cool on a rack.

*Matcha green tea powder, which is very high in antioxidants, is used in the Japanese tea ceremony. White chocolate softens the bitterness. This cookie is the perfect introduction to matcha.*

# MATCHA OAT

preparation: 20 minutes + baking: 15 minutes

**makes 25 cookies**
225 g (8 oz/1 cup) unsalted butter,
   at room temperature
220 g (7¾ oz/packed 1 cup) light
   brown sugar
110 g (4 oz/½ cup) caster
   (superfine) sugar
2 eggs
270 g (10 oz/2 cups) plain
   (all-purpose) flour
1 teaspoon bicarbonate of soda
   (baking soda)
1 teaspoon salt
12 g (6 teaspoons) matcha
120 g (4 oz/1¼ cups) rolled oats

Preheat the oven to 160°C (320°F/Gas mark 3).
Cream the butter and sugars until well blended. Incorporate
the eggs, then the flour, bicarbonate of soda, salt, matcha
and oats.
Form the dough into balls about the size of a golf ball and
space them about 7 cm (2¾ in) apart on a baking sheet.
Bake for 15 minutes. Leave the cookies to rest on the baking
sheet for 5 minutes and then allow to cool on a rack.

*I created this cookie for the Taiwanese restaurant Zen Zoo
near the Opéra district of Paris. It has twice the amount of matcha
as the previous recipe, so it's perfect for matcha lovers.*

# PISTACHIO

**makes 25 cookies**

225 g (8 oz/1 cup) slightly salted
  butter, at room temperature
100 g (3¼ oz) pistachio paste
300 g (11 oz/packed 1½ cups)
  light brown sugar
150 g (5 oz/⅔ cup) caster
  (superfine) sugar
2 large eggs
550 g (1 lb 3 oz/4¼ cups) plain
  (all-purpose) flour
2 teaspoons bicarbonate of soda
  (baking soda)
1 teaspoon salt
40–50 pistachios, halved

Preheat the oven to 160°C (320°F/Gas mark 3).
Cream the butter, pistachio paste and sugars until well
blended. Incorporate the eggs, then the flour, bicarbonate
of soda and salt.
Form the dough into balls about the size of a golf ball and
space them about 7 cm (2¾ in) apart on a baking sheet.
Top each ball with 3–4 pistachio halves.
Bake for 10 minutes. Leave the cookies to rest on the baking
sheet for 5 minutes and then allow to cool on a rack.

*My French father-in-law loves pistachio desserts.*
*So here is a pistachio-rich recipe for cookies that look*
*every bit as good as they taste!*

# CAFÉ

preparation: 20 minutes + baking: 15 minutes

**makes 25 cookies**

225 g (8 oz/1 cup) slightly salted butter, at room temperature

150 g (5 oz/packed ¾ cup) dark brown sugar

50 g (2 oz/packed ¼ cup) light brown sugar

90 g (3¼ oz/⅓ cup) caster (superfine) sugar

2 eggs

6 teaspoons coffee extract

375 g (13 oz/2¾ cups) plain (all-purpose) flour

1 teaspoon bicarbonate of soda (baking soda)

10 g (½ oz) ground coffee

½ teaspoon salt

140 g (5 oz) dark cooking (baking) chocolate, chopped or in discs

Preheat the oven to 160°C (320°F/Gas mark 3).
Cream the butter and sugars until well blended. Incorporate the eggs and coffee extract, then the flour, bicarbonate of soda, coffee and salt. When the mixture is smooth, stir in the chocolate.
Form the dough into balls the size of a golf ball and space them about 7 cm (2¾ in) apart on a baking sheet.
Bake for 15 minutes. Leave the cookies to rest on the baking sheet for 5 minutes and then allow to cool on a rack.

*A coffee-flavoured cookie to dunk . . . in your coffee!*

# ALMOND

preparation: 20 minutes + baking: 12 minutes

**makes 16–18 cookies**
185 g (6½ oz/¾ cup) unsalted
  butter, at room temperature
105 g (3½ oz/packed ½ cup) light
  brown sugar
60 g (2 oz/¼ cup) caster
  (superfine) sugar
1 egg
1 teaspoon almond extract
220 g (7¾ oz/1¾ cup) plain
  (all-purpose) flour
30 g (1 oz/¼ cup) ground
  almonds
1 teaspoon bicarbonate of soda
  (baking soda)
½ teaspoon salt
white sesame seeds, for coating
flaked almonds, for decoration

Preheat the oven to 160°C (320°F/Gas mark 3).
Cream the butter and sugars until well blended. Incorporate the egg and almond extract, then the flour, ground almonds, bicarbonate of soda and salt. The dough must be smooth and well blended.
Form the dough into balls the size of a golf ball and roll them in the sesame seeds to coat them.
Space them about 7 cm (2¾ in) apart on a baking sheet.
Top each ball with a few flaked almonds.
Bake for 12 minutes. Leave the cookies to rest on the baking sheet for 5 minutes and then allow to cool on a rack.

*A Chinese almond cookie that I have made softer in texture*
*thanks to the magic of brown sugar.*

# GWENOLA KISS

preparation: 30 minutes + baking: 8 minutes

**makes 20 cookies**
40 g (1½ oz/scant ¼ cup)
  unsalted butter
225 g (8 oz) dark cooking (baking)
  chocolate, chopped or in discs
2 large eggs
120 g (4 oz/½ cup) caster
  (superfine) sugar
60 g (2¼ oz/½ cup) plain
  (all-purpose) flour
1 teaspoon bicarbonate of soda
  (baking soda)
1 teaspoon salt
90 g (3¼ oz) caramel milk
  chocolate, chopped
good quality sea salt flakes

Preheat the oven to 175°C (350°F/Gas mark 4).
Melt the butter and dark cooking chocolate in a saucepan over a gentle heat, stirring regularly. Leave to cool for a few minutes.
Beat the eggs and sugar together until smooth. Incorporate the chocolate-butter mixture, then the flour, bicarbonate of soda and salt. When the dough is smooth, stir in the caramel chocolate.
Form the dough into balls the size of a golf ball using two spoons and space them about 7 cm (2¾ in) apart on a baking sheet.
Bake for 8 minutes. Take the cookies out of the oven and sprinkle each one with a little salt 'kiss'. Leave the cookies to rest on the baking sheet for 5 minutes and then allow to cool on a rack.

*This 'kiss' is a salted kiss! Its intense chocolate dough is liquidy and can't be kept in the fridge or freezer.*

# CARAMBAR®

preparation: 25 minutes + baking: 15 minutes

**makes 25 cookies**

12 Carambars® (the original)
225 g (8 oz/1 cup) unsalted butter,
   at room temperature
100 g (3½ oz/packed ½ cup) dark
   brown sugar
100 g (3½ oz/packed ½ cup) light
   brown sugar
90 g (3¼ oz/⅓ cup) caster
   (superfine) sugar
2 eggs
1 teaspoon vanilla extract
400 g (14 oz/3 cups) plain
   (all-purpose) flour
1 teaspoon bicarbonate of soda
   (baking soda)
1 teaspoon salt

Preheat the oven to 160°C (320°F/Gas mark 3).
Heat the Carambars® on a plate in the microwave for
10–15 seconds. Cut each Carambar® into ten equal pieces
with scissors.
Cream the butter and sugars until well blended. Incorporate
the eggs and the vanilla extract, then the flour, bicarbonate
of soda and salt.
Form the dough into balls the size of a golf ball. Push
4–5 pieces of Carambar® into each ball, and then reshape.
Space them about 7 cm (2¾ in) apart on a baking sheet.
Bake for 15 minutes. Leave the cookies to rest on the baking
sheet for 5 minutes and then allow to cool on a rack.

*Carambar® is a brand of traditional French caramel sweet (candy).*
*You can replace with a caramel or toffee sweet. Just cut*
*the pieces in little chunks for this cookie.*

# HONEY

preparation: 20 minutes + baking: 10 minutes

**makes 25 cookies**

225 g (8 oz/1 cup) unsalted butter,
  at room temperature
300 g (11 oz) runny honey
80 g (3 oz/packed ⅓ cup) light
  brown sugar
25 g (1 oz/2 tablespoons)
  caster (superfine) sugar,
  plus a little for coating
450 g (1 lb/3⅓ cups) plain
  (all-purpose) flour
1 teaspoon bicarbonate of soda
  (baking soda)
¼ teaspoon salt

Preheat the oven to 160°C (320°F/Gas mark 3).
Cream the butter, honey and sugars until well blended.
Incorporate the flour, bicarbonate of soda and salt until
the dough is smooth.
Form the dough into balls the size of a golf ball then roll
in sugar to coat them. Arrange them as you go on a baking
sheet spaced 7 cm (2¾ in) apart.
Bake for 10 minutes. Leave the cookies to rest on the baking
sheet for 5 minutes and then allow to cool on a rack.

*I like the eucalyptus honey of Miel & Une Nuit – the owners are
friends of mine who hunt for the best honeys from around the
world. Use your favourite runny honey for this recipe.*

# PEANUT BUTTER

preparation: 25 minutes + baking: 9 minutes

**makes 25 cookies**

225 g (8 oz/1 cup) unsalted
butter, at room temperature
110 g (3¾ oz/½ cup) peanut
butter
300 g (10½ oz/packed 1¼ cups)
light brown sugar
200 g (7 oz/¾ cup) caster
(superfine) sugar, plus a little
for decorating
2 eggs
1 teaspoon vanilla extract
440 g (15½ oz/3¼ cups) plain
(all-purpose) flour
1 teaspoon bicarbonate of soda
(baking soda)
1 teaspoon salt
50 peanuts, halved

Preheat the oven to 175°C (350°F/Gas mark 4).
Cream the butter, peanut butter and sugars until well
blended. Incorporate the eggs and the vanilla extract,
then the flour, bicarbonate of soda and salt until the dough
is smooth and even.
Form the dough into balls the size of a golf ball and top each
one with 3–4 peanut halves, pressing them in lightly. Reshape
the balls and space them about 7 cm (2¾ in) apart on a
baking sheet. Moisten a fork with water. Dip it into a bowl
of sugar. Make diagonal hash marks across each ball, pressing
lightly. This is the famous peanut butter cookie mark!
Bake for 9 minutes. Leave the cookies to rest on the baking
sheet for 5 minutes and then allow to cool on a rack.

*Another classic. Note: this cookie is even better
if you can grind your own peanut butter.*

# LEMON MACADAMIA

preparation: 20 minutes + baking: 15 minutes

### makes 25 cookies

110 g (3¾ oz/½ cup) salted
  butter, at room temperature
110 g (3¾ oz/½ cup)
  Philadelphia® cream cheese
225 g (8 oz/packed 1¼ cups) light
  brown sugar
110 g (3¾ oz/½ cup) caster
  (superfine) sugar
1 large egg
2 teaspoons pure lemon extract
zest of 1 lemon
350 g (12⅓ oz/2¾ cups) plain
  (all-purpose) flour
1 teaspoon bicarbonate of soda
  (baking soda)
1 small pinch of salt
175 g (6 oz) macadamia
  nuts, whole

Preheat the oven to 160°C (320°F/Gas mark 3).
Cream the butter, cream cheese and sugars until well blended.
Incorporate the egg, lemon extract and zest, then the flour,
bicarbonate of soda and salt. When the dough is smooth, stir
in the macadamia nuts.
Form the dough into balls the size of a golf ball and space
them about 7 cm (2¾ in) apart on a baking sheet.
Bake for 15 minutes. Leave the cookies to rest on the baking
sheet for 5 minutes and then allow to cool on a rack.

*I was inspired by a recipe created by Mrs Fields®, the queen
of cookies in the United States. Her cookie book was one
of the very first cookery books I collected.*

36 **CLASSICS**

# SNICKERDOODLE

preparation: 20 minutes + baking: 10 minutes

**makes 25 cookies**

110 g (4 oz/½ cup) unsalted
 butter, at room temperature
110 g (4 oz/½ cup) margarine,
 at room temperature
360 g (12 oz/1½ cups) caster
 (superfine) sugar
1 teaspoon bicarbonate of soda
 (baking soda)
2 eggs
370 g (13 oz/2¾ cups)
 plain (all-purpose) flour
2 teaspoons cream of tartar
1 teaspoon salt
1 teaspoon cinnamon mixed with
 3 tablespoons sugar, for coating

Preheat the oven to 175°C (350°F/Gas mark 4).
Cream the butter, margarine and sugar until well blended.
Incorporate the bicarbonate of soda and eggs, then the flour,
cream of tartar and salt.
Form the dough into balls the size of a golf ball and roll
them in the sugar-cinnamon mixture. Space them about
7 cm (2¾ in) apart on a baking sheet.
Bake for 10 minutes. Leave the cookies to rest on the baking
sheet for 5 minutes and then allow to cool on a rack.

*My favourite childhood cookie – the touch of cinnamon is magical
in this classic American recipe! Mrs Klingler, from my home town in
Kansas, gave me the secret: mix half butter and half margarine.*

# SSEB

preparation: 30 minutes + baking: 15 minutes

**makes 25 cookies**

115 g (4 oz/½ cup) salted
  butter
115 g (4 oz) dark cooking (baking)
  chocolate, chopped or in discs
2 large eggs
350 g (12 oz/1¼ cups) caster
  (superfine) sugar
150 g (5 oz/1¼ cups) plain
  (all-purpose) flour
½ teaspoon bicarbonate of soda
  (baking soda)
50 g (2 oz/½ cup) cocoa powder
½ teaspoon salt
90 g (3¼ oz) dark cooking (baking)
  chocolate in chunks or pieces
½ teaspoon Thai (bird's eye) chilli
  flakes or chilli powder

Preheat the oven to 160°C (320°F/Gas mark 3).
Melt the butter and dark chocolate in a saucepan over a
gentle heat, stirring regularly. Leave to cool for a few minutes.
Beat the eggs and sugar together until smooth. Incorporate
the chocolate-butter mixture, then the flour, bicarbonate of
soda, cocoa powder and salt. When the dough is smooth,
incorporate the chocolate pieces and chilli.
Form the dough into balls the size of a golf ball and space
them about 7 cm (2¾ in) apart on a baking sheet.
Bake for 15 minutes. Leave the cookies to rest on the baking
sheet for 5 minutes and then allow to cool on a rack.

*This is one of my favourite cookies. It contains dried Thai chilli*
*and dark chocolate. Sseb is a Thai word that means*
*'delicious and spicy', so it's a perfect name.*

# BEER

preparation: 25 minutes + baking: 15 minutes

**makes 25 cookies**

225 g (8 oz/1 cup) salted butter, at room temperature
200 g (7 oz/packed ¾ cup) light brown sugar
80 g (3 oz/⅓ cup) caster (superfine) sugar
50 g (2 oz) maple syrup
2 eggs
1 teaspoon vanilla extract
80 g (3 oz) fresh brewer's spent grain, plus 20 g (¾ oz) mixed with 1 tablespoon maple syrup
350 g (12 oz/2⅔ cups) plain (all-purpose) flour
1 teaspoon bicarbonate of soda (baking soda)
1 teaspoon salt

Preheat the oven to 160°C (320°F/Gas mark 3).
Cream the butter, sugars and maple syrup until well blended.
Incorporate the eggs, vanilla extract and spent grain, then the flour, bicarbonate of soda and salt.
Form the dough into balls the size of a golf ball. Space them about 7 cm (2¾ in) apart on a baking sheet, and top each one with a little of the maple syrup mixture.
Bake for 15 minutes. Leave the cookies to rest on the baking sheet for 5 minutes and then allow to cool on a rack.

*I created this cookie for my neighbour Brew Unique, the first Parisian atelier where you can brew your own beer. Spent grain is the leftover malt from the brewing process.*

# MOJO

**makes 25 cookies**
225 g (8 oz/1 cup) unsalted butter,
    at room temperature
200 g (7 oz/packed ¾ cup)
    light brown sugar
90 g (3¼ oz/⅓ cup) caster
    (superfine) sugar
2 eggs
zest and juice of 1 lime
15 g (½ oz) chopped fresh mint
400 g (14 oz/3 cups) plain
    (all-purpose) flour
1 teaspoon bicarbonate of soda
    (baking soda)
1 teaspoon salt
1 drop of green food colouring
green-coloured sugar, for coating
rum, for coating

Preheat the oven to 150°C (300°F/Gas mark 2).
Cream the butter and sugars until well blended. Incorporate the eggs, lime zest and juice as well as the mint, then the flour, bicarbonate of soda and salt. When the dough is smooth, stir in the food colouring.
Form the dough into balls the size of a golf ball and roll them in the green sugar. Space them about 7 cm (2¾ in) apart on a baking sheet.
Bake for 12 minutes. Leave the cookies to rest on the baking sheet for 5 minutes and then allow to cool on a rack.
Once cooled, brush the surface of each cookie with rum using a pastry brush or small spoon.

*I love mojitos, so a mojito cookie was a personal challenge!*
*The fresh mint, lime and rum are nicely balanced in this recipe.*

# GINGER

preparation: 25 minutes + baking: 12 minutes

**makes 25 cookies**
225 g (8 oz/1 cup) slightly salted
 butter, at room temperature
200 g (7 oz/packed ¾ cup) light
 brown sugar
90 g (3¼ oz/⅓ cup) caster
 (superfine) sugar
2 eggs
1 teaspoon ground ginger
1 tablespoon freshly grated ginger
400 g (14 oz/3 cups) plain
 (all-purpose) flour
1 teaspoon bicarbonate of soda
 (baking soda)
1 teaspoon salt
75 g (2½ oz) stem (candied)
 ginger, diced

Preheat the oven to 160°C (320°F/Gas mark 3).
Cream the butter and sugars until well blended. Incorporate the eggs and ground and grated ginger, then the flour, bicarbonate of soda and salt. When the dough is smooth, stir in the diced stem ginger.
Form the dough into balls the size of a golf ball and space them about 7 cm (2¾ in) apart on a baking sheet.
Bake for 12 minutes. Leave the cookies to rest on the baking sheet for 5 minutes and then allow to cool on a rack.

*Stem ginger, ground ginger and freshly grated
ginger, all in one recipe. Another one of my favourites!*

# CRAN'N BERRY

preparation: 20 minutes + baking: 15 minutes

**makes 25 cookies**
225 g (8 oz/1 cup) slightly salted
    butter, at room temperature
180 g (6½ oz/packed ¾ cup) light
    brown sugar
75 g (2½ oz/⅓ cup) caster
    (superfine) sugar
2 eggs
1 teaspoon vanilla extract
350 g (12 oz/2⅔ cups) plain
    (all-purpose) flour
1 teaspoon bicarbonate of soda
    (baking soda)
1 teaspoon salt
50 g (2 oz) white chocolate,
    chopped
50 g (2 oz/½ cup) dessicated
    (shredded) coconut, plus a little
    for coating
50 g (2 oz/scant ½ cup) dried
    cranberries

Preheat the oven to 160°C (320°F/Gas mark 3).
Cream the butter and sugars until well blended. Incorporate the eggs and the vanilla extract, then the flour, bicarbonate of soda and salt. When the dough is smooth, stir in the white chocolate, coconut and cranberries.
Form the dough into balls the size of a golf ball. Roll them in the shredded coconut. Space them about 7 cm (2¾ in) apart on a baking sheet.
Bake for 15 minutes. Leave the cookies to rest on the baking sheet for 5 minutes and then allow to cool on a rack.

*The white chocolate, cranberry and coconut form
a super trio: sweet, sour and texture. My youngest son, Luc,
thought of this funny name for the cookie.*

# VALENTINE

preparation: 30 minutes + baking: 15 minutes

**makes 25 cookies**
115 g (4 oz/½ cup) salted
  butter
115 g (4 oz) Valrhona Guanaja
  70% dark chocolate (or other
  dark chocolate)
2 large eggs
350 g (12 oz/1¼ cups) caster
  (superfine) sugar
½ teaspoon bicarbonate of soda
  (baking soda)
½ teaspoon salt
150 g (5 oz/1¼ cups) plain
  (all-purpose) flour
50 g (2 oz/½ cup)
  cocoa powder
25 raspberries, squashed

Preheat the oven to 160°C (320°F/Gas mark 3).
Melt the butter and chocolate in a saucepan over a gentle heat, stirring regularly. Leave to cool for a few minutes.
Whisk the eggs and sugar. Stir in the chocolate-butter mixture until smooth. Stir in the bicarbonate of soda, salt, flour and cocoa powder.
Form the dough into balls the size of a golf ball and space them about 7 cm (2¾ in) apart on a baking sheet. Push your thumb gently into each one and insert a squashed raspberry. Bake for 15 minutes. Leave the cookies to rest on the baking sheet for 5 minutes and then allow to cool on a rack.
Spread the cooked raspberry over the surface of the cookie with a teaspoon.

*Valentine works at Valrhona's headquarters,
and I created this cookie for her, using Valrhona's
Guanaja 70% dark chocolate and fresh raspberries.*

# CHOCO PECAN CRANBERRY

preparation: 30 minutes + baking: 15 minutes

**makes 25 cookies**
115 g (4 oz/½ cup) slightly
 salted butter
115 g (4 oz) dark cooking (baking)
 chocolate, chopped or in discs
2 large eggs
350 g (12 oz/1¼ cups) caster
 (superfine) sugar
½ teaspoon bicarbonate of soda
 (baking soda)
½ teaspoon salt
150 g (5 oz/1¼ cups) plain
 (all-purpose) flour
50 g (2 oz/½ cup) cocoa powder
50 g (2 oz) crushed pecans
50 g (2 oz/½ cup) dried
 cranberries

Preheat the oven to 160°C (320°F/Gas mark 3).
Melt the butter and dark chocolate in a saucepan over
a gentle heat, stirring regularly. Leave to cool for a few minutes.
Whisk the eggs and sugar then pour in the chocolate-butter
and mix until smooth. Incorporate the bicarbonate of soda,
salt, flour and cocoa powder, then the pieces of pecans
and cranberries.
Form the dough into balls the size of a golf ball and space
them about 7 cm (2¾ in) apart on a baking sheet.
Bake for 15 minutes. Leave the cookies to rest on the baking
sheet for 5 minutes and then allow to cool on a rack.

*The base of the dough is the same as the Triple C (see page 12).*
*It's a fabulous base to create your own recipes.*

# M&M'S®

preparation: 20 minutes + baking: 15 minutes

**makes 25 cookies**
225 g (8 oz/1 cup) salted butter,
    at room temperature
200 g (7 oz/packed ¾ cup) light
    brown sugar
90 g (3¼ oz/⅓ cup) caster
    (superfine) sugar
2 eggs
1 teaspoon vanilla extract
400 g (14 oz/3 cups) plain
    (all-purpose) flour
1 teaspoon bicarbonate of soda
    (baking soda)
1 teaspoon salt
100 g (3½ oz) M&M's®

Preheat the oven to 160°C (320°F/Gas mark 3).
Cream the butter and sugars until well blended. Incorporate the eggs and the vanilla extract, then the bicarbonate of soda, salt and flour. The dough must be smooth and even. Stir in the M&M's®.
Form the dough into balls the size of a golf ball and space them about 7 cm (2¾ in) apart on a baking sheet.
Bake for 15 minutes. Leave the cookies to rest on the baking sheet for 5 minutes and then allow to cool on a rack.

*For the 'kid' in all of us, this cookie is fun and easy*
*for children to make! Use plain milk chocolate M&M's®.*

# DOMINO

preparation: 25 minutes + baking: 13 minutes

**makes 20 cookies**
175 g (6 oz/¾ cup) unsalted butter,
  at room temperature
75 g (2½ oz/¼ cup) peanut butter
150 g (5 oz/packed ⅔ cup) light
  brown sugar
50 g (2 oz/¼ cup) caster
  (superfine) sugar
2 eggs
1 teaspoon vanilla extract
100 g (3½ oz/½ cup)
  rice flour
125 g (4⅓ oz/¾ cup)
  buckwheat flour
25 g (¾ oz/¼ cup) cornflour
  (cornstarch)
1 teaspoon bicarbonate of soda
  (baking soda)
½ teaspoon salt
50 g (2 oz) chocolate chips
20 g (¾ oz) crushed peanuts

Preheat the oven to 175°C (350°F/Gas mark 4).
Cream the butter, peanut butter and sugars until well blended. Incorporate the eggs and vanilla extract, then the flours, cornflour (cornstarch), bicarbonate of soda and salt. When the dough is smooth, stir in the chocolate chips and peanuts.
Form the dough into balls the size of a golf ball and space them about 7 cm (2¾ in) apart on a baking sheet.
Bake for 13 minutes. Leave the cookies to rest on the baking sheet for 5 minutes and then allow to cool on a rack.

*Named after a chic client who wanted a good gluten-free cookie... what Domino wants, she gets!*

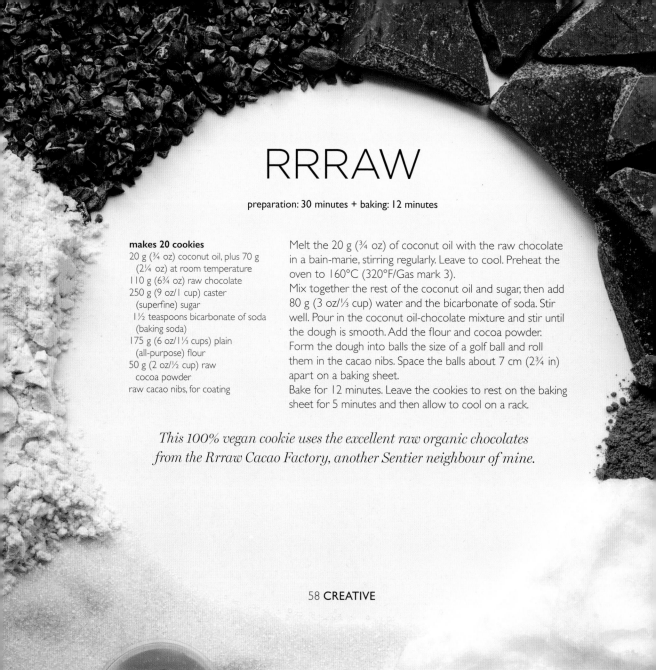

# RRRAW

preparation: 30 minutes + baking: 12 minutes

**makes 20 cookies**
20 g (¾ oz) coconut oil, plus 70 g
  (2¼ oz) at room temperature
110 g (6¾ oz) raw chocolate
250 g (9 oz/1 cup) caster
  (superfine) sugar
1½ teaspoons bicarbonate of soda
  (baking soda)
175 g (6 oz/1⅓ cups) plain
  (all-purpose) flour
50 g (2 oz/½ cup) raw
  cocoa powder
raw cacao nibs, for coating

Melt the 20 g (¾ oz) of coconut oil with the raw chocolate in a bain-marie, stirring regularly. Leave to cool. Preheat the oven to 160°C (320°F/Gas mark 3).

Mix together the rest of the coconut oil and sugar, then add 80 g (3 oz/⅓ cup) water and the bicarbonate of soda. Stir well. Pour in the coconut oil-chocolate mixture and stir until the dough is smooth. Add the flour and cocoa powder.

Form the dough into balls the size of a golf ball and roll them in the cacao nibs. Space the balls about 7 cm (2¾ in) apart on a baking sheet.

Bake for 12 minutes. Leave the cookies to rest on the baking sheet for 5 minutes and then allow to cool on a rack.

*This 100% vegan cookie uses the excellent raw organic chocolates from the Rrraw Cacao Factory, another Sentier neighbour of mine.*

# VANILLA X

preparation: 25 minutes + chilling: 1 hour + baking: 12 minutes

### makes 20 cookies
115 g (4 oz/½ cup) slightly salted
   butter, at room temperature
100 g (3½ oz/½ cup) vegetable oil
1 tablespoon vanilla extract
120 g (4 oz/½ cups) caster
   (superfine) sugar
70 g (2¼ oz/½ cup) icing
   (confectioner's) sugar
1 large egg
300 g (11 oz/2½ cups) plain
   (all-purpose) flour
1 teaspoon bicarbonate of soda
   (baking soda)
½ teaspoon salt

### for the glaze
225 g (8 oz/1 cup) icing
   (confectioner's) sugar
3–4 tablespoons milk
1 vanilla pod (bean)

Preheat the oven to 160°C (320°F/Gas mark 3).
Cream the butter, oil, vanilla extract and caster sugar until
well blended. Incorporate the icing sugar, then the egg and
finally the flour, bicarbonate of soda and salt. Chill in the
refrigerator for 1 hour.
Form the dough into balls the size of a golf ball and space
them about 7 cm (2¾ in) apart on a baking sheet.
Bake for 12 minutes. Leave the cookies to rest on the baking
sheet for 5 minutes and then allow to cool on a rack.
When the cookies have cooled, prepare the glaze. Mix the
icing sugar and milk with a fork. The consistency should be
slightly runny. If necessary add ½ tablespoon of milk. Split the
vanilla pod, scrape out the seeds and stir them into the glaze.
Place some kitchen paper under the cookie rack. Dip the
top of each cookie in the glaze. Place them on the rack
and leave to set for 15 minutes.

*The vanilla dessert created by Pierre Hermé for the Royal
Monceau Hotel inspired me to make an eXtreme vanilla cookie.*

# GINGERBREAD

preparation: 40 minutes + chilling: 2 hours + baking: 10 minutes

**makes 60–70 cookies**
225 g (8 oz/1 cup) unsalted butter,
    at room temperature
300 g (11 oz/1 cup) caster
    (superfine) sugar
200 g (7 oz) molasses
1 egg
600 g (1 lb 5 oz/4 cups) plain
    (all-purpose) flour
1 teaspoon bicarbonate of soda
    (baking soda)
1 teaspoon salt
1 tablespoon cocoa powder
1 tablespoon ground ginger
2 teaspoons ground cloves
2 teaspoons cinnamon

**for the glaze**
1 egg white
450 g (1 lb/4½ cups) icing
    (confectioner's) sugar
½ tablespoon lemon juice

Cream the butter, sugar and molasses until well blended. Incorporate the egg, then the rest of the ingredients. Divide the dough into 3 portions and wrap in cling film (plastic wrap). Chill in the refrigerator for at least 2 hours.
Preheat the oven to 175°C (350°F/Gas mark 4).
On a lightly floured work surface, roll out each ball of dough to a thickness of 3 mm. Cut out the cookies with a pastry cutter and arrange on baking sheets.
Bake for 10 minutes. Leave the cookies to rest on the baking sheet for 5 minutes and then allow to cool on a rack.
For the glaze, mix the ingredients with 3 tablespoons water. The mixture should be smooth and not lumpy, and neither too runny nor too thick. Add a little water or icing sugar as needed. Put the glaze in a piping bag with a 2–3 mm nozzle. Decorate the gingerbread men to bring them to life!

*These gingerbread people fill the shop
with a delicious aroma every December.*

# GLAZED SUGAR COOKIES

preparation: 40 minutes + chilling: 2 hours + baking: 10 minutes

**makes 60–70 cookies**
225 g (8 oz/1 cup) unsalted butter,
   at room temperature
400 g (14 oz/1½ cups) caster
   (superfine) sugar
2 eggs
2 teaspoons vanilla extract
575 g (1 lb 4 oz/4 cups) plain
   (all-purpose) flour
2 teaspoons baking powder
1 teaspoon salt

**for the glaze**
2 egg whites
900 g (2 lbs/9 cups) icing
   (confectioner's) sugar
1 tablespoon lemon juice
food colourings of your choice

Cream the butter and sugar until well blended. Incorporate the eggs and vanilla extract, then the rest of the ingredients. Divide the dough into 3 portions and wrap in cling film (plastic wrap). Chill in the refrigerator for at least 2 hours. Preheat the oven to 175°C (350°F/Gas mark 4).
On a lightly floured work surface, roll out each ball of dough to a thickness of 3 mm. Cut out the cookies with a pastry cutter and arrange on baking sheets.
Bake for 10 minutes. Leave the cookies to rest on the baking sheet for 5 minutes and then allow to cool on a rack.
For the glaze, mix the ingredients with a fork. The mixture should be smooth and not lumpy, and neither too runny nor too thick. Add up to 6 tablespoons water or icing sugar as needed. Divide the glaze into small bowls and add the chosen colours. Put each glaze in a piping bag with a 2–3 mm nozzle and decorate the cookies.

*At Christmas, our neighbours would give us plates of delicious cookies. The glazed sugar cookie was my favourite.*

# COOKIE SHOT

preparation: 50 minutes + baking: 10 minutes

**makes 20 shots**
60 g (2 oz/¼ cup) slightly salted
  butter, at room temperature
50 g (2 oz/¼ cup) dark brown
  sugar
2 tablespoons caster (superfine)
  sugar
½ egg, beaten
½ teaspoon vanilla extract
1 small pinch of bicarbonate
  of soda (baking soda)
1 small pinch of salt
90 g (3¼ oz/¾ cup) plain
  (all-purpose) flour
30 g (1 oz) chocolate chips

**for the cocktail**
500 ml (17 fl oz/2 cups)
  almond milk
500 ml (17 fl oz/2 cups) rum
4 tablespoons maple syrup

Preheat the oven to 160°C (320°F/Gas mark 3).
Cream the butter and sugars until well blended. Add the egg and vanilla extract, bicarbonate of soda, salt and flour. Once well combined, stir in the chocolate chips.
Form the dough into 20 balls the size of a hazelnut and space them about 7cm (2¾ in) apart on a baking sheet.
Bake for 10 minutes. When the cookies are ready, take them out of the oven and immediately cut slits into each one so that they can be served on a glass. Leave the cookies to rest on the baking sheet for 5 minutes and then allow to cool on a rack.
Mix the almond milk, rum and maple syrup. Pour the cocktail into shot glasses. Pop one cookie onto each glass… party time!

*I had the idea of a real 'cookie shot' dunking in your*
*mini cookie then downing the shot. My neighbour Joseph, of Mabel*
*Cocktail Den, created this simple and perfect cocktail.*

# MATCHA
## ICE CREAM COOKIE SANDWICH

preparation: 40 minutes + chilling: overnight + freezing: 2 hours

**makes 15 ice cream
cookie sandwiches**
30 Matcha Oat cookies (page 20)

**for the matcha ice cream**
1 litre (34 fl oz/4 cups) whole
  (full-fat) milk
200 ml (7 fl oz/¾ cup) light double
  (heavy) cream
20 g (¾ oz) matcha
150 g (5 oz) egg yolks
  (approximately 7–9 eggs)
150 g (5 oz/¾ cup) caster
  (superfine) sugar

Heat the milk and cream in a saucepan. As soon as it starts to boil, remove from the heat and pour in the matcha. Whisk gently before setting aside.

In a bowl, whisk the egg yolks and sugar until creamy and pale in colour. Bring the matcha-milk mixture back up to the boil. Gently pour over the egg yolks. Stir and return to the saucepan over a low heat. Cook this custard, stirring continuously with a wooden spoon, until it coats the spoon (83°C/181°F with a food thermometer).

Transfer the custard to a container, cover with cling film (plastic wrap) and leave in the refrigerator overnight.

Pour the custard into an ice-cream maker and churn for 20–30 minutes. Freeze in an airtight container for 2 hours. Take two cookies of the same size and insert one scoop of ice cream between them with the tops of the cookies facing outwards. Press the cookies to spread the ice cream to the edges.

*I use organic matcha from Jugetsudo for all my
matcha recipes. Matcha lovers, rejoice!*

68 EXTRAS

# VANILLA
## ICE CREAM COOKIE SANDWICH

preparation: 40 minutes + chilling: overnight + freezing: 2 hours

**makes 15 ice cream
cookie sandwiches**
30 Arthur cookies (page 8)

**for the vanilla ice cream**
4 vanilla pods (beans)
1 litre (34 fl oz/4 cups) whole
  (full-fat) milk
200 ml (7 fl oz/1 cup) light
  whipping cream
150 g (5 oz) egg yolks
  (approximately 7–9 eggs)
150 g (5 oz/¾ cup) caster
  (superfine) sugar

Split the vanilla pods and scrape out the seeds. Heat the milk, cream, vanilla seeds and pods in a saucepan. When it starts to boil, remove from the heat and cover with cling film (plastic wrap). Leave to infuse for 30 minutes.
Whisk the egg yolks and sugar until creamy and pale in colour. Strain the vanilla milk, return it to the saucepan and bring back up to the boil. Gently pour over the egg yolks. Stir and return to the saucepan over a low heat. Cook the custard, stirring continuously with a wooden spoon. It is ready when the custard coats the spoon (83°C/181°F with a food thermometer). Transfer the custard into a container, cover with cling film and leave in the refrigerator overnight. Pour the custard into an ice-cream maker and churn for 20–30 minutes. Freeze in an airtight container for 2 hours. Take two cookies and insert one scoop of ice cream between them with the tops of the cookies facing outwards. Press the cookies to spread the ice cream to the edges.

## ACKNOWLEDGEMENTS

Thank you to my hubby Philippe and to my three kids, Noëmie, Angelin and Luc for helping me embark on this great adventure: developing the project of having a cookie business, coming up with creative ideas, hand rolling hundreds (thousands!) of cookies, cleaning my shop and correcting my French. You have always helped me without any complaints. Mama love! Many thanks also to the Hwang Carrant families, our many friends, my assistants, our devoted clients and to Marabout for your precious help, support and appetites!

A big thank you to Nathalie and Le Ruban Vert, the very first restaurant I baked for; to Akiko for her beautiful photos and to Kanako for her icing skills. And thank you to chefs Adeline, Eddy, Daniel (all three of you!), Greg and to Mr Hermé for your appreciation of my cookies and support right from the beginning.

Cookie love forever! *Jean*

**Boutique Jean Hwang Carrant**
84, rue d'Aboukir
75002 Paris, France

www.jeanhwangcarrant.com
Facebook: Jean Hwang Carrant
Instagram: jeanhwangcarrant

First published by Hachette Livre (Marabout) in 2018
This English language edition published in 2019 by Hardie Grant Books, an imprint of Hardie Grant Publishing

Hardie Grant Books (London)
5th & 6th Floors, 52–54 Southwark Street
London SE1 1UN

Hardie Grant Books (Melbourne)
Building 1, 658 Church Street
Richmond, Victoria 3121

hardiegrantbooks.com

British Library Cataloguing-in-Publication Data. A catalogue record for this book is available from the British Library.

Cookie Love by Jean Hwang Carrant
ISBN: 978-1-78488-258-7

For the French edition:
Designer: Sophie Villette
Proofreaders: Sabrina Bendersky and Natacha Kotchetkova
Photographer: Akiko Ida

For the English edition:
Publishing Director: Kate Pollard
Junior Editor: Eila Purvis
Editor: Eve Marleau
Translator: Gilla Evans
Typesetter: David Meikle

Cover reproduction: p2d
Printed and bound in China by Leo Paper Group